Obama's Islamization of America

By

Will Clark

Obama's
Islamization
of
America

ISBN-13: 978-1508863090
ISBN-10: 1508863091

Published by
Motivation Basics
P.O. Box 6327
Diamondhead, MS 39525
Will01@aol.com

For more information about the author
visit
AuthorsDen.com

QUOTE

"A nation can survive its fools, and even the ambitious. But it cannot survive treason from within. An enemy at the gates is less formidable, for he is known and carries his banner openly. But the traitor moves amongst those within the gate freely, his sly whispers rustling through all the alleys, heard in the very halls of government itself. For the traitor appears not a traitor; he speaks in accents familiar to his victims, and he wears their face and their arguments, he appeals to the baseness that lies deep in the hearts of all men. He rots the soul of a nation, he works secretly and unknown in the night to undermine the pillars of the city, he infects the body politic so that it can no longer resist. A murderer is less to fear. The traitor is the plague." *Marcus Tullius Cicero, 58 B.C. Speech in the Roman Senate*

Contents

Article	Page
Introduction	7
Memorandum	10
The Document	14
Obama's Support	36
Education	52
Islamization	72
Conclusion	78
About the Author	79
Never Forget	81
Greatest Quotes	83
Other Books by the Author	85

Introduction

Is Barack Obama, the man elected to defend and protect our great nation, America, determined to destroy it? His actions and words give a clear and definitive answer to that question. Not only is he not fulfilling that sacred trust and responsibility; at this time he is the man most responsible for destroying America. His words and deeds spew blasphemy and deception without end. Blasphemy and deception are words used throughout the Bible to describe the one most dangerous to Christians and the stability of the entire world.

Is he the one described in the Bible Book of Revelation as the 'Beast;' or the one often spoken of and described as the Antichrist in other parts of the Bible? Perhaps we will not know the answer to this question until that time arrives. However, at this time he seems the one best positioned, with the greatest following, and demonstrating the best example of that prophesied person of destruction. Many indications reveal he has great appeal to fulfill that destined role in history, especially Biblical history.

Heretofore, America has been guided by many leaders, some great and some not so great. Until now, regardless of their abilities, they were all guided by one commonality. To some degree, all those leaders professed a belief in God as our Creator. Each also recognized that higher authority as the foundation of our nation's place offering hope and opportunity for all humanity, even those living outside our nation.

Suddenly, Barack Obama came into power, from obscurity, and changed our fundamental guiding light. He erased that Christian and positive commonality by suddenly proclaiming, "We are no longer a Christian nation." Although he meekly claims to be a 'Christian' his words, deeds, and actions clearly demonstrate without any doubt whatsoever that he is not as he says. A Christian would never utter such deep blasphemies routinely spewing from his lips.

With that statement, he disrupted the foundation of our being and our guiding beacon. While Christians stood fast, he deceived his many followers with his great words of blasphemy. They followed him as if he were their newly arrived savior. They didn't ask where they were being led. They questioned nothing of his goals or his intentions. He said 'Trust me' and they laid down their inhibitions and their souls to be trampled upon by one not guided by concern for their future happiness or salvation.

They were guided by his words of blasphemy and deceit and followed him onto a precipitous ledge of human disaster. With their eyes and ears closed they helped him carry us to that great danger. (Revelation 2:7, "He that hath an ear, let him hear what the Spirit saith unto the churches...)

With this background as a starting place, we must consider where Barack Obama plans to take us into the future. It's certainly not the place our Founding Fathers planned and designed for us. It's not the road to independence, happiness, and salvation. It's more a road so often tread throughout history into peril, disaster, and inhumanity. In this case, it's into a place ruled by the dictates of Islamic terror veiled as the 'Religion of Peace.'

Presently, America faces three evil and determined threats. First is that of anarchy and socialism as described and guided by Saul

Alinsky. Barack Obama and Hillary Clinton are fervent supporters
and advocates of his policies and 'rules.' Hillary Clinton even had
direct contact and correspondence with Alinsky while she was a
college student. Her correspondence showed her support for his
proclamations. One of her personal letters to him is still posted on
the internet.

Obama was too young to know Alinsky personally, nevertheless
he was greatly influenced by his writings. He even taught the
'Alinsky Rules for Radicals' while he was a community organizer,
particularly while he was in the Gamaliel organization. Members
of the Gamaliel group are the ones who once prayed, "Deliver us,
Obama!" Is this not recognition of a false messiah?

The second potential assault on our great nation is that of fear; fear
of direct attacks by terrorists on our soil. Of course, if that fear
becomes deep enough Obama will certainly use that to impose
more dictatorial control by proclaiming martial law to 'control
terrorism.' As I have emphasized in many of my writings; every
competent American citizen **must** be armed to discourage
terrorists from setting foot upon our soil. Every citizen must not
only be allowed to own a defensive weapon; they should be
required to own a weapon. Of course, Obama and his minions, his
'Useful Idiots,' will continue their efforts to disarm American
citizens.

This writing addresses only the third attack on America. This is
the most insidious and likely the most devastating to America's
survival. This danger is presented by the Muslim Brotherhood, and
is most often described as the 'Third Jihad' or the 'Silent Jihad.'
It's the Muslim plan to transition America, and the West, totally
into Islam through a process or a plan called 'Settlement.' It's
already here; their plan is working; their plan is in writing and they
are throwing it right in the faces of unaware American citizens.

Obama is even helping them accomplish their goal. Is he part of the process; is he really a leading member of the Muslim Brotherhood to accomplish that plan? That detailed plan titled, **"An Explanatory Memorandum On the General Strategic Goal for the Group In North America"** will be described next.

The Memorandum

In this effort described in the Memorandum, Muslims have a long-range plan to transpose America into a total Islamic country "without firing a single shot." It's from a Muslim Brotherhood plan discovered in 1991, titled, 'An Explanatory Memorandum: On the General Strategic Goal for the Group In North America.' Just take a casual look around and you will see how far they have already progressed in this effort. Many Islamists connected to the Muslim Brotherhood are already in powerful positions in our government - including important advisory positions to the President of the United States. This article from discoverthenetworks.org gives an overview of the plan:

"In July 2007, seven key leaders of an Islamic charity known as the Holy Land Foundation for Relief and Development (HLF) went on trial for charges that they had: (a) provided "material support and resources" to a foreign terrorist organization (namely Hamas); (b) engaged in money laundering; and (c) breached the International Emergency Economic Powers Act, which prohibits transactions that threaten American national security. Along with the seven named defendants, the U.S. government released a list of approximately 300 "unindicted co-conspirators" and "joint venturers." During the course of the HLF trial, many incriminating documents were entered into evidence. Perhaps the most significant of these was "An Explanatory Memorandum on the General Strategic Goal for the Group in North America," by the Muslim Brotherhood operative Mohamed Akram. Federal investigators found Akram's memo in the home of Ismael Elbarasse, a founder of the Dar Al-Hijrah mosque in Falls Church, Virginia, during a 2004 search. Elbarasse was a member of the Palestine Committee, which the Muslim Brotherhood had created to support Hamas in the United States.

Written sometime in 1987 but not formally published until May 22, 1991, Akram's 18-page document listed the Brotherhood's 29 likeminded "organizations of our friends" that shared the common goal of dismantling American institutions and turning the U.S. into a Muslim nation. These "friends" were identified by Akram and the Brotherhood as groups that could help convince Muslims "that their work in America is a kind of grand Jihad in eliminating and destroying the Western civilization from within and 'sabotaging' its miserable house by their hands ... so that ... God's religion [Islam] is made victorious over all other religions."

Akram was well aware that in the U.S., it would be extremely difficult to promote Islam by means of terror attacks. Thus the "grand jihad" that he and his Brotherhood comrades envisioned was not a violent one involving bombings and shootings, but rather a stealth (or "soft") jihad aiming to impose Islamic law (Sharia) over every region of the earth by incremental, non-confrontational means, such as working to "expand the observant Muslim base"; to "unif[y] and direc[t] Muslims' efforts"; and to "present Islam as a civilization alternative." At its heart, Akram's document details a plan to conquer and Islamize the United States – not as an ultimate objective, but merely as a stepping stone toward the larger goal of one day creating "the global Islamic state."

In line with this objective, Akram and the Brotherhood resolved to "settle" Islam and the Islamic movement within the United States, so that the Muslim religion could be "enabled within the souls, minds and the lives of the people of the country." Akram explained that this could be accomplished "through the establishment of firmly-rooted organizations on whose bases civilization, structure and testimony are built." He urged Muslim leaders to make "a shift from the collision mentality to the absorption mentality," meaning that they should abandon any tactics involving defiance or confrontation, and seek instead to implant into the larger society a host of seemingly benign Islamic groups with ostensibly unobjectionable motives; once those groups had gained a measure of public acceptance, they would be in a position to more effectively promote societal transformation by the old Communist technique of "boring from within."

"The heart and the core" of this strategy, said Akram, was contingent upon these groups' ability to develop "a mastery of the art of 'coalitions.'" That is, by working synergistically they could complement, augment, and amplify one another's efforts. Added Akram: "The big challenge that is ahead of us is how to turn these seeds or 'scattered' elements into comprehensive, stable, 'settled' organizations that are connected with our Movement and which fly in our orbit and take orders from our guidance." The ultimate objective was not only an enlarged Muslim presence, but also implementation of the Brotherhood objectives of transforming pluralistic societies, particularly America, into Islamic states, and sweeping away Western notions of legal equality, freedom of conscience, freedom of religion, and freedom of speech.

Akram and the Brotherhood understood that in order to succeed in this endeavor, they needed to appeal to different strata of the American population in different ways; that whereas some people could be influenced by messages delivered from a religious perspective, others would be more responsive to messages delivered by educators, or bankers, or political figures, or journalists, etc. Thus, Akram's blueprint for the advancement of the Islamic movement stressed the need to form a coalition of groups coming from the worlds of education; religious proselytization; political activism; audio and video production; print media; banking and finance; the physical sciences; the social sciences; professional and business networking; cultural affairs; the publishing and distribution of books; children and teenagers; women's rights; vocational concerns; and jurisprudence.

By promoting the Islamic movement on such a wide variety of fronts, the Brotherhood and its allies could multiply exponentially their influence. Toward that end, the Akram/Brotherhood "Explanatory Memorandum" named the following 29 groups as the organizations they believed could collaborate effectively to destroy America from within – "if they all march according to one plan." End of article. This is that plan. It begins:

In the name of God, the Beneficent, the Merciful Thanks be to God, Lord of the Two Worlds, Prayers and peace be upon the master of the Messengers.

The Document

An Explanatory Memorandum
On the General Strategic Goal for the Group In North America
5/22/1991

Contents:
1- An introduction in explanation
2- The Concept of Settlement
3- The Process of Settlement
4- Comprehensive Settlement Organizations

The beloved brother/The General Masul, may God keep him.

The beloved brother/Secretary of the Shura Council, may God keep him.

The beloved brothers/Members of the Shura Council, may God keep them.

God's peace, mercy and blessings be upon you.... To proceed.

I ask Almighty God that you, your families and those whom you love around you are in the best of conditions, pleasing to God, glorified His name be.

I send this letter of mine to you hoping that it would seize your attention and receive your good care as you are the people of responsibility and those to whom trust is given. Between your hands is an "Explanatory Memorandum" which I put effort in writing down so that it is not locked in the chest and the mind, and so that I can share with you a portion of the responsibility in leading the Group in this country.

What might have encouraged me to submit the memorandum in this time in particular is my feeling of a "glimpse of hope" and the beginning of good tidings which bring the good news that we have embarked on a new stage of Islamic activism stages in this continent. The papers which are between your hands are not abundant extravagance, imaginations or hallucinations which passed in the mind of one of your brothers, but they are rather hopes, ambitions and challenges that I hope that you share some or most of which with me. I do not claim their infallibility or absolute correctness, but they are an attempt which requires study, outlook, detailing and rooting from you.

My request to my brothers is to read the memorandum and to write what they wanted of comments and corrections, keeping in mind that what is between your hands is not strange or a new submission without a root, but rather an attempt to interpret and explain some of what came in the long-term plan which we approved and adopted in our council and our conference in the year (1987).

So, my honorable brother, do not rush to throw these papers away due to your many occupations and worries. All what I'm asking of you is to read them and to comment on them hoping that we might continue together the project of our plan and our Islamic work in this part of the world. Should you do that, I would be thankful and grateful to you.

I also ask my honorable brother, the Secretary of the Council, to add the subject of the memorandum on the Council agenda in its coming meeting.

God, the Beneficent, the Merciful Thanks be to God, Lord of the Two Worlds And Blessed are the Pious.

Subject: A project for an explanatory memorandum for the General Strategic goal for the Group in North America mentioned in the long-term plan

One: The Memorandum is derived from:

1- The general strategic goal of the Group in America which was approved by the Shura Council and the Organizational Conference for the year [1987] is "Enablement of Islam in North America, meaning: establishing an effective and a stable Islamic Movement led by the Muslim Brotherhood which adopts Muslims' causes domestically and globally, and which works to expand the observant Muslim base, aims at unifying and directing Muslims' efforts, presents Islam as a civilization alternative, and supports the global Islamic State wherever it is."

2- The priority that is approved by the Shura Council for the work of the Group in its current and former session which is "Settlement".

3- The positive development with the brothers in the Islamic Circle in an attempt to reach a unity of merger.

4- The constant need for thinking and future planning, an attempt to read it and working to "shape" the present to comply and suit the needs and challenges of the future.

5- The paper of his eminence, the General Masul, may God keep him, which he recently sent to the members of the Council.

Two: An Introduction to the Explanatory Memorandum:

In order to begin with the explanation, we must "summon" the following question and place it in front of our eyes as its relationship is important and necessary with the strategic goal and the explanation project we are embarking on. The question we are facing is: "How do you like to see the Islam Movement in North America in ten years?", or "taking along" the following sentence when planning and working, "Islamic Work in North America in the year (2000): A Strategic Vision".

Also, we must summon and take along "elements" of the general strategic goal of the Group in North America and I will intentionally repeat them in numbers. They are:

1. Establishing an effective and stable Islamic Movement led by the Muslim Brotherhood.

2. Adopting Muslims' causes domestically and globally.

3. Expanding the observant Muslim base.

4. Unifying and directing Muslims' efforts.

5. Presenting Islam as a civilization alternative

6. Supporting the establishment of the global Islamic State wherever it is.

It must be stressed that it has become clear and emphatically known that all is in agreement that we must "settle" or "enable" Islam and its Movement in this part of the world. Therefore, a joint understanding of the meaning of settlement or enablement must be adopted, through which and on whose basis we explain the general strategic goal with its six elements for the Group in North America.

Three: The Concept of Settlement:

This term was mentioned in the Group's "dictionary" and documents with various meanings in spite of the fact that everyone meant one thing with it. We believe that the understanding of the essence is the same and we will attempt here to give the word and its "meanings" a practical explanation with a practical Movement tone, and not a philosophical linguistic explanation, while stressing that this explanation of ours is not complete until our explanation of "the process" of settlement itself is understood which is mentioned in the following paragraph. We briefly say the following:

Settlement: "That Islam and its Movement become a part of the homeland it lives in". Establishment: "That Islam turns into firmly-rooted organizations on whose bases civilization, structure and testimony are built". Stability: "That Islam is stable in the land on which its people move". Enablement: "That Islam is enabled within the souls, minds and the lives of the people of the country in which it moves". Rooting: "That Islam is resident and not a passing thing, or rooted "entrenched" in the soil of the spot where it moves and not a strange plant to it".

Four : The Process of Settlement:

In order for Islam and its Movement to become "a part of the homeland" in which it lives, "stable" in its land, "rooted" in the spirits and minds of its people, "enabled" in the live of its society and has firmly-established "organizations" on which the Islamic structure is built and with which the testimony of civilization is achieved, the Movement must plan and struggle to obtain "the keys" and the tools of this process in carry out this grand mission as a "Civilization Jihadist" responsibility which lies on the shoulders of Muslims and - on top of them - the Muslim Brotherhood in this country. Among these keys and tools are the following:

1- Adopting the concept of settlement and understanding its practical meanings:

The Explanatory Memorandum focused on the Movement and the realistic dimension of the process of settlement and its practical meanings without paying attention to the difference in understanding between the resident and the non-resident, or who is the settled and the non-settled and we believe that what was mentioned in the long-term plan in that regards suffices.

2- Making a fundamental shift in our thinking and mentality in order to suit the challenges of the settlement mission.

What is meant with the shift - which is a positive expression - is responding to the grand challenges of the settlement issues. We believe that any transforming response begins with the method of thinking and its center, the brain, first. In order to clarify what is meant with the shift as a key to qualify us to enter the field of settlement, we say very briefly that the following must be accomplished:

A shift from the partial thinking mentality to the comprehensive thinking mentality.

A shift from the "amputated" partial thinking mentality to the "continuous" comprehensive mentality.

A shift from the mentality of caution and reservation to the mentality of risk and controlled liberation.

A shift from the mentality of the elite Movement to the mentality of the popular Movement.

A shift from the mentality of preaching and guidance to the mentality of building and testimony.

A shift from the single opinion mentality to the multiple opinion mentality.

A shift from the collision mentality to the absorption mentality.

A shift from the individual mentality to the team mentality.

A shift from the anticipation mentality to the initiative mentality.

A shift from the hesitation mentality to the decisiveness mentality.

A shift from the principles mentality to the programs mentality.

A shift from the abstract ideas mentality the true organizations mentality [This is the core point and the essence of the memorandum].

3- Understanding the historical stages in which the Islamic Ikhwani activism went through in this country:

The writer of the memorandum believes that understanding and comprehending the historical stages of the Islamic activism which was led and being led by the Muslim Brotherhood in this continent is a very important key in working towards settlement, through which the Group observes its march, the direction of its movement and the curves and turns of its road. We will suffice here with mentioning the title for each of these stages [The title expresses the prevalent characteristic of the stage] [Details maybe mentioned in another future study]. Most likely, the stages are:

A- The stage of searching for self and determining the identity.

B- The stage of inner build-up and tightening the organization.

C- The stage of mosques and the Islamic centers.

D- The stage of building the Islamic organizations - the first phase.

E- The stage of building the Islamic schools - the first phase.

F- The stage of thinking about the overt Islamic Movement - the first phase.

G- The stage of openness to the other Islamic movements and attempting to reach a formula for dealing with them - the first phase.

H- The stage of reviving and establishing the Islamic organizations - the second phase.

We believe that the Group is embarking on this stage in its second phase as it has to open the door and enter as it did the first time.

4-Understanding the role of the Muslim Brother in North

America:

The process of settlement is a "Civilization-Jihadist Process" with all the word means. The Ikhwan must understand that their work in America is a kind of grand Jihad in eliminating and destroying the Western civilization from within and "sabotaging" its miserable house by their hands and the hands of the believers so that it is eliminated and God's religion is made victorious over all other religions. Without this level of understanding, we are not up to this challenge and have not prepared ourselves for Jihad yet. It is a Muslim's destiny to perform Jihad and work wherever he is and wherever he lands until the final hour comes, and there is no escape from that destiny except for those who chose to slack. But, would the slackers and the Mujahedeen be equal.

5-Understanding that we cannot perform the settlement mission by ourselves or away from people:

A mission as significant and as huge as the settlement mission needs magnificent and exhausting efforts. With their capabilities, human, financial and scientific resources, the Ikhwan will not be able to carry out this mission alone or away from people and he who believes that is wrong, and God knows best. As for the role of the Ikhwan, it is the initiative, pioneering, leadership, raising the banner and pushing people in that direction. They are then to work to employ, direct and unify Muslims' efforts and powers for this process. In order to do that, we must possess a mastery of the art of "coalitions", the art of "absorption" and the principles of "cooperation".

6-The necessity of achieving a union and balanced gradual merger between private work and public work:

We believe that what was written about this subject is many and is enough. But, it needs a time and a practical frame so that what is needed is achieved in a gradual and a balanced way that is compatible with the process of settlement.

7-The conviction that the success of the settlement of Islam and its Movement in this country is a success to the global Islamic Movement and a true support for the sought-after state, God willing:

There is a conviction - with which this memorandum disagrees - that our focus in attempting to settle Islam in this country will lead to negligence in our duty towards the global Islamic Movement in supporting its project to establish the state. We believe that the reply is in two segments: One - The success of the Movement in America in establishing an observant Islamic base with power and effectiveness will be the best support and aid to the global Movement project. And the second - is the global Movement has not succeeded yet in "distributing roles" to its branches, stating what is the needed from them as one of the participants or contributors to the project to establish the global Islamic state. The day this happens, the children of the American Ikhwani branch will have far-reaching impact and positions that make the ancestors proud.

8-Absorbing Muslims and winning them with all of their factions and colors in America and Canada for the settlement project, and making it their cause, future and the basis of their Islamic life in this part of the world:

This issues requires from us to learn "the art of dealing with the others", as people are different and people in many colors. We need to adopt the principle which says, "Take from people... the best they have", their best specializations, experiences, arts, energies and abilities. By people here we mean those within or

23

without the ranks of individuals and organizations. The policy of "taking" should be with what achieves the strategic goal and the settlement process. But the big challenge in front of us is: how to connect them all in "the orbit" of our plan and "the circle" of our Movement in order to achieve "the core" of our interest. To me, there is no choice for us other than alliance and mutual understanding of those who desire from our religion and those who agree from our belief in work. And the U.S. Islamic arena is full of those waiting...., the pioneers.

What matters is bringing people to the level of comprehension of the challenge that is facing us as Muslims in this country, conviction of our settlement project, and understanding the benefit of agreement, cooperation and alliance. At that time, if we ask for money, a lot of it would come, and if we ask for men, they would come in lines. What matters is that our plan is "the criterion and the balance" in our relationship with others.

Here, two points must be noted; the first one: we need to comprehend and understand the balance of the Islamic powers in the U.S. arena [and this might be the subject of a future study]. The second point: what we reached with the brothers in "ICNA" is considered a step in the right direction, the beginning of good and the first drop that requires growing and guidance.

9-Re-examining our organizational and administrative bodies, the type of leadership and the method of selecting it with what suits the challenges of the settlement mission:

The memorandum will be silent about details regarding this item even though it is logical and there is a lot to be said about it,

10-Growing and developing our **resources and capabilities,** our

financial and human resources with what suits the magnitude of the grand mission:

If we examined the human and the financial resources the Ikhwan alone own in this country, we and others would feel proud and glorious. And if we add to them the resources of our friends and allies, those who circle in our orbit and those waiting on our banner, we would realize that we are able to open the door to settlement and walk through it seeking to make Almighty God's word the highest.

11-Utilizing the scientific method in planning, thinking and preparation of studies needed for the process of settlement:

Yes, we need this method, and we need many studies which aid in this civilization Jihadist operation. We will mention some of them briefly:

The history of the Islamic presence in America. The history of the Islamic Ikhwani presence in America. Islamic movements, organizations and organizations: analysis and criticism. The phenomenon of the Islamic centers and schools: challenges, needs and statistics. Islamic minorities, Muslim and Arab communities.

The U.S. society: make-up and politics. The U.S. society's view of Islam and Muslims... And many other studies which we can direct our brothers and allies to prepare, either through their academic studies or through their educational centers or organizational tasking. What is important is that we start.

12-Agreeing on a flexible, balanced and a clear "mechanism" to implement the process of settlement within a specific, gradual and balanced "time frame" that is in-line with the demands and challenges of the process of settlement.

13-Understanding the U.S. society from its different aspects an understanding that "qualifies" us to perform the mission of settling our Dawa' in its country "and growing it" on its land.

14-Adopting a written "jurisprudence" that includes legal and movement bases, principles, policies and interpretations which are suitable for the needs and challenges of the process of settlement.

15-Agreeing on "criteria" and balances to be a sort of "antennas" or "the watch tower" in order to make sure that all of our priorities, plans, programs, bodies, leadership, monies and activities march towards the process of the settlement.

16-Adopting a practical, flexible formula through which our central work complements our domestic work. (Items 12 through 16 will be detailed later.)

17-Understanding the role and the nature of work of "The Islamic Center" in every city with what achieves the goal of the process of settlement:

The center we seek is the one which constitutes the "axis" of our Movement, the "perimeter" of the circle of our work, our "balance center", the "base" for our rise and our "Dar al-Arqam" to educate us, prepare us and supply our battalions in addition to being the "niche" of our prayers.

This is in order for the Islamic center to turn - in action not in words - into a seed "for a small Islamic society" which is a reflection and a mirror to our central organizations. The center ought to turn into a "beehive" which produces sweet honey. Thus, the Islamic center would turn into a place for study, family, battalion, course, seminar, visit, sport, school, social club, women gathering, kindergarten for male and female youngsters, the office of the domestic political resolution, and the center for distributing our newspapers, magazines, books and our audio and visual tapes.

In brief we say: we would like for the Islamic center to become "The House of Dawa'" and "the general center" in deeds first before name. As much as we own and direct these centers at the continent level, we can say we are marching successfully towards the settlement of Dawa' in this country.

Meaning that the "center's" role should be the same as the "mosque's" role during the time of God's prophet, God's prayers and peace be upon him, when he marched to "settle" the Dawa' in its first generation in Madina. from the mosque, he drew the Islamic life and provided to the world the most magnificent and fabulous civilization humanity knew.

This mandates that, eventually, the region, the branch and the Usra turn into "operations rooms" for planning, direction, monitoring and leadership for the Islamic center in order to be a role model to be followed.

18-Adopting a system that is based on "selecting" workers, "role distribution" and "assigning" positions and responsibilities is based on specialization, desire and need with what achieves the process of settlement and contributes to its success.

19-Turning the principle of dedication for the Masuls of main positions within the Group into a rule, a basis and a policy in work. Without it, the process of settlement might be stalled [Talking about this point requires more details and discussion].

20-Understanding the importance of the "Organizational" shift in our Movement work, and doing Jihad in order to achieve it in the real world with what serves the process of

settlement and expedites its results, God Almighty's willing:

The reason this paragraph was delayed is to stress its utmost importance as it constitutes the heart and the core of this memorandum. It also constitutes the practical aspect and the true measure of our success or failure in our march towards settlement. The talk about the organizations and the "organizational" mentality or phenomenon does not require much details. It suffices to say that the first pioneer of this phenomenon was our prophet Mohamed, God's peace, mercy and blessings be upon him, as he placed the foundation for the first civilized organization which is the mosque, which truly became "the comprehensive organization".

And this was done by the pioneer of the contemporary Islamic Dawa', Imam martyr Hasan al-Banna, may God have mercy on him, when he and his brothers felt the need to "re-establish" Islam and its movement anew, leading him to establish organizations with all their kinds: economic, social, media, scouting, professional and even the military ones. We must say that we are in a country which understands no language other than the language of the organizations, and one which does not respect or give weight to any group without effective, functional and strong organizations.

It is good fortune that there are brothers among us who have this "trend", mentality or inclination to build the organizations who have beat us by action and words which leads us to dare say honestly what Sadat in Egypt once said, "We want to build a country of organizations" - a word of right he meant wrong with. I say to my brothers, let us raise the banner of truth to establish right "We want to establish Group organizations", as without it we will not able to put our feet on the true path.

And in order for the process of settlement to be completed, we must plan and work from now to equip and prepare ourselves, our brothers, our apparatuses, our sections and our committees in order to turn into comprehensive organizations in a gradual and balanced way that is suitable with the need and the reality. What encourages us to do that - in addition to the aforementioned -is that we possess "seeds" for each organization from the organization we call for.

All we need is to tweak them, coordinate their work, collect their elements and merge their efforts with others and then connect them with the comprehensive plan we seek.

For instance, We have a seed for a "comprehensive media and art" organization: we own a print + advanced typesetting machine + audio and visual center + art production office + magazines in Arabic and English [The Horizons, The Hope, The Politicians, Ha Falastine, Press Clips, al-Zaytouna, Palestine Monitor, Social Sciences Magazines...] + art band + photographers + producers + programs anchors + journalists + in addition to other media and art experiences". Another example:

We have a seed for a "comprehensive Dawa' educational" organization: We have the Daw'a section in ISNA + Dr. Jamal Badawi Foundation + the center run by brother Hamed al-Ghazali + the Dawa' center the Dawa' Committee and brother Shaker al-Sayyed are seeking to establish now + in addition to other Daw'a efforts here and there...". And this applies to all the organizations we call on establishing.

The big challenge that is ahead of us is how to turn these seeds or "scattered" elements into comprehensive, stable, "settled" organizations that are connected with our Movement and which fly in our orbit and take orders from our guidance. This does not prevent - but calls for - each central organization to have its local branches but its connection with the Islamic center in the city is a must.

What is needed is to seek to prepare the atmosphere and the means to achieve "the merger" so that the sections, the committees, the regions, the branches and the Usras are eventually the heart and the core of these organizations. Or, for the shift and the change to occur as follows:

1- The Movement Department + The Secretariat Department
2- Education Department + Dawa'a Com.
3- Sisters Department
4- The Financial Department + Investment Committee + The Endowment
5- Youth Department + Youths Organizations Department
6- The Social Committee + Matrimony Committee + Mercy Foundation
7- The Security Committee
8- The Political Depart. + Palestine Com.
9- The Group's Court + The Legal Com.
10-Domestic Work Department
11- Our magazines + the print + our art band
12- The Studies Association + The Publication House + Dar al-Kitab
13- Scientific and Medial societies
14- The Organizational Conference
15- The Shura Council + Planning Com.
16- The Executive Office
17- The General Masul
18- The regions, branches & Usras

The **Organizational & Administrative Organization**
The General Center

Dawa' and Educational Organization
The Women's Organization
The Economic Organization
Youth Organizations
The Social Organization
The Security Organization
The Political Organization
The Judicial Organization
Its work is to be distributed to the rest of the organizations
The Media and Art Organization
The Intellectual & Cultural Organization
Scientific, Educational & Professional Organization
The Islamic-American Founding Conference
The Shura Council for the Islamic-American Movement
The Executive Office of the Islamic-American Movement
Chairman of the Islamic Movement and its official Spokesman
Field leaders of organizations & Islamic centers

Five: Comprehensive Settlement Organization:

We would then seek and struggle in order to make each one of these above-mentioned organizations a "comprehensive organization" throughout the days and the years, and as long as we are destined to be in this country. What is important is that we put the foundation and we will be followed by peoples and generations that would finish the march and the road but with a clearly-defined guidance.

And, in order for us to clarify what we mean with the comprehensive, specialized organization, we mention here the characteristics and traits of each organization of the "promising" organizations.

1-From the Dawa' and educational aspect [The Dawa* and

Educational Organization]: to include:

The Organization to spread the Dawa' (Central and local branches).
An institute to graduate Callers and Educators.
Scholars, Callers, Educators, Preachers and Program Anchors.
Art and communication technology, Conveyance and Dawa'.
A television station.
A specialized Dawa' magazine.
A radio station.
The Higher Islamic Council for Callers and Educators.
The Higher Council for Mosques and Islamic Centers.
Friendship Societies with the other religions... and things like that.

2-Politically [The Political Organization]: to include:

A central political party.
Local political offices.
Political symbols.
Relationships and alliances.
The American Organization for Islamic Political Action
Advanced Information Centers....and things like that.

3-Media [The Media and Art Organization]: to include:

A daily newspaper,
Weekly, monthly and seasonal magazines.
Radio stations.
Television programs.
Audio and visual centers.
A magazine for the Muslim child.
A magazine for the Muslim woman.
A print and typesetting machines.
A production office.

A photography and recording studio
Art bands for acting, chanting and theater.
A marketing and art production office... and things like that.

4-Economically [The Economic Organization!: to include:

An Islamic Central bank.
Islamic endowments.
Investment projects.
An organization for interest-free loans.... and things like that.

5-Scientifically and Professionally [The Scientific. Educational and Professional Organization]: to include:

Scientific research centers.
Technical organizations and vocational training.
An Islamic university.
Islamic schools.
A council for education and scientific research.
Centers to train teachers.
Scientific societies in schools.
An office for academic guidance.
A body for authorship and Islamic curricula.... and things like that.

6-Culturally and Intellectually [The Cultural and Intellectual Organization]: to include:

A center for studies and research.
Cultural and intellectual foundations such as [The Social Scientists Society - Scientists and Engineers Society....].
An organization for Islamic thought and culture.
A publication, translation and distribution house for Islamic books.
An office for archiving, history and authentication
The project to translate the Noble Quran, the Noble Sayings....and

things like that.

7-Socially [The Social-Charitable Organization]: to include:

Social clubs for the youths and the community's sons and daughters.
Local societies for social welfare and the services are tied to the Islamic centers.
The Islamic Organization to Combat the Social Ills of the U.S. Society.
Islamic houses project.
Matrimony and family cases office....and things like that.

8-Youths [The Youth Organization!: to include:

Central and local youths foundations.
Sports teams and clubs
Scouting teams....and things like that.

9-Women [The Women Organization]: to include:

Central and local women societies.
Organizations of training, vocational and housekeeping.
An organization to train female preachers.
Islamic kindergartens...and things like that.

10-Organizationally and Administratively [The Administrative and Organizational Organization!: to include:

An institute for training, growth, development and planning
Prominent experts in this field
Work systems, bylaws and charters fit for running the most complicated bodies and organizations
A periodic magazine in Islamic development and administration.

Owning camps and halls for the various activities.
A data, polling and census bank.
An advanced communication network.
An advanced archive for our heritage and production....and things like that.

11-Security [The Security Organization!: to include:

Clubs for training and learning self-defense techniques.
A center which is concerned with the security issues [Technical, intellectual, technological and human]....and things like that.

12-Legally [The Legal Organization]: to include:

A Central Jurisprudence Council.
A Central Islamic Court.
Muslim Attorneys Society.
The Islamic Foundation for Defense of Muslims' Rights...and things like that. And success is by God.

Attachment

A list of our organizations and the organizations of our friends [Imagine if they all march according to one plan!!!]

AMSE	The Association of Muslim Scientists and Engineers
IMA	Islamic Medical Association
ITC	Islamic Teaching Center
NAIT	North American Islamic Trust
FID	Foundation for International Development
IHC	Islamic Housing Cooperative
ICD	Islamic Centers Division
ATP	American Trust Publications

AVC	Audio-Visual Center
IBS	Islamic Book Service
MBA	Muslim Businessmen Association
MYNA	Muslim Youth of North America
IFC	ISNA Fiqh Committee
IPAC	ISNA Politial Awareness Committee
IED	Islamic Education Department
MAYA	Muslim Arab Youth Association
MISG	Malasian Islamic Study Group
IAP	Islamic Association for Palestine
UASR	United Association for Studies and Research
OLF	Occupied Land Fund
MIA	Mercey International Association
ICNA	Islamic Circle of North America
BMI	Baitul Mal Inc.
IIIT	International Institute for Islamic Thought
IIC	Islamic Information Center

Obama's Direct Support

This is the Islamic plan for their 'Silent Jihad.' It's already well-advanced in our nation. And, too many are turning their backs and closing their eyes; and closing their ears not to see it, hear it, or understand it. Our national leaders are not only refusing to challenge this silent Jihad, they seem to be encouraging it and supporting it - even financially. This is only one example:

Obama strongly supported Morsi, of the Muslim Brotherhood, as the president of Egypt, refusing to offer support to Egypt when Morsi was overthrown. Following is an example of his support to the Muslim Brotherhood - the architect of that plan to destroy the

United States from within. It involves a large sum of money offered to Morsi. This report from mrconservative.com by Kristin Tate gives that information:

"Secretary of State John Kerry secretly gave $1.3 billion to Egypt, which is controlled by the Muslim Brotherhood. (This was before the Muslim Brotherhood's Morsi was ousted by the military.)

To give this "gift", Kerry had to waive restrictions put in place by Congress, which forbid giving US military aid unless the country meets certain basic democracy standards. The secretary of state is supposed to certify that the recipient country's government is "supporting the transition to civilian government, including holding free and fair elections, implementing policies to protect freedom of expression, association and religion, and due process of law."

Muslims are also testing their encroachment with their terrorist fear tactic combined with their 'settlement' plan. An example is their rising 'no-go' zones. This is an article published on Jan 15, 2015 by ETV NEWS. It was reported in a newsletter from Martin Mawyer, Jan. 15, 2015, from the Christian Action Network:

"In the wake of the horrific slaughter at the Charlie Hebdo magazine office in France, the media is suddenly interested in Islamic "no-go" zones scattered throughout Europe where many Muslims are radicalized into jihadists.

But it's important for Americans to understand that right here in the United States we have real "no-go" zones that have been in existence for decades.

On Wednesday I appeared on the Fox and Friends show to discuss America's Islamic no-go zones with host Brian Kilmeade. I explained that a group of Muslims known as Muslims of America (MOA) has as many as two dozen enclaves scattered around the nation, including in Virginia, California, Georgia, South Carolina and New York.

MOA was founded by a Pakistani cleric, Sheikh Mubarik Gilani, and are also known as Jamaat al Fuqra (community of the impoverished).

Several years ago, when my camera crew attempted to enter one of the enclaves in Red House, Virginia, we were angrily and violently forced to leave. Some of the enclaves, including the ones located in Hancock, N.Y., and York, S.C., have entrances protected by armed guards.

The no-go zones that exist right now in America are even more dangerous than the European ones which are so much in the news today. Throughout the al Fuqra camps in the United States, members conduct weapons training and shooting drills. This doesn't happen in the European no-go zones.

And in the U.S. enclaves, they even receive instruction in guerilla combat, how to strangle an enemy and cut a throat. All of these activities have been captured on video.

They exist in remote, rural, often mountainous regions of America where detection is difficult. When they shoot their guns or conduct drills, there is often no one within earshot to hear.

Al Fuqra was once listed on the State Department's watch list of terror organizations – yet today it operates on dozens of enclaves as independent no-go zones with no interference from the outside world. The camps have their own government, with their own mayors and town councils. And because they are Muslim, they use

Islamic Sharia law to govern their day-to-day operations."

There are also many Islamists already positioned, according to their 'settlement' plan, that silent jihad, in Obama's administration. This conundrum of confusion allows Obama to shift back and forth so he can't be tied to either - either which is a direct threat to the perpetuation of our democracy. But, these are good Muslims - not radical Muslims. They worship from the same written source document, so that means when they destroy all non-Muslims, they will do it in a kinder, gentler way. Perhaps they will use a sharper sword than the radical Muslims, who will use a dull sword.

They are deceiving the world, and Barack Obama is their greatest promoter. Is he part of them; or is he using them merely as a distraction while he ventures onward toward his self-perceived destiny of dictatorship? Who knows for sure? In either case, according to the Memorandum, he has appointed many prominent Muslims to high positions in his administration. Only six of his most prominent appointments are shown next, but they are typical of his many Muslim appointments to help design the future of our nation. The investigativeproject.org is only one of many organizations that identifies these six:

Arif Alikhan – Assistant Secretary for Policy Development for the U.S. Department of Homeland Security. Arif Alikhan played a key role in the removal of the LAPD "Mapping" Plan which involved mapping Muslim communities in an effort to identify potential hotbeds of extremism. LAPD officials said that it was crucial for them to gain a better understanding of isolated parts of the Muslim community because those groups can potentially breed violent extremism.

Alikhan reportedly helped raise funds for Muslim Public Affairs

Council (MPAC) that has labeled a deadly anti-U.S. terrorist attack a legitimate operation, referred to terrorists as "freedom fighters" and equated Muslim jihad with the sentiments of American statesman Patrick Henry. He joined MPAC on April 11 for a special fundraiser called "Be the Change" to support what the group calls its innovative leadership development programs.

Mohammed Elibiary – Homeland Security Adviser. According to information reported in an article by the Investigative Project on Terrorism, Mohamed Elibiary has defended Muslim Brotherhood luminary Sayyid Qutb, Ayatollah Khomeini, and radical New York Imam Siraj Wahhaj. He has asserted conspiracy theories, supported terror-related individuals and organizations and accused the government of mounting a war against Islam. Despite all this, he was appointed by Department of Homeland Security (DHS) Secretary Janet Napolitano to the Homeland Security Advisory Council (HSAC).

Elibiary is the co-founder, president and CEO of the Freedom and Justice Foundation (F&J), founded in November 2002 "to promote a Centrist Public Policy environment in Texas by coordinating the state level government and interfaith community relations for the organized Texas Muslim community." F&J's nonprofit status was revoked by the IRS in May 2010 for failure to file the requisite 990 forms that would reveal the entity's source of income. Similarly, according to the Texas Comptroller of Public Accounts, F&J has not filed a Texas Franchise Tax Public Information Report.

The North Texas Islamic Council (NTIC), also called the "Texas Islamic Council," is an affiliate organization of F&J. Elibiary is the registered agent for the NTIC, and one of the directors is H. Mustafaa Carroll, who is also the executive director of the Houston chapter of the Council on American-Islamic Relations

(CAIR). CAIR is a Muslim Brotherhood-linked group in the U.S. that was formed as part of a Hamas-support network in the U.S. Elibiary was a Fellow in 2008-2009 with the American Muslim Civic Leadership Institute (AMCLI), "housed at the University of Southern California's Center for Religion and Civic Culture (CRCC), which works in partnership with the Prince Alwaleed Bin Talal Center for Muslim Christian Understanding (ACMCU) at Georgetown University." This is the center where Obama had the Christian icon covered with black plywood before he made his speech there in April, 2009.

Elibiary was featured in a CNN piece in December 2009 as a "deradicalizer." He likened the allure of radicalism among American Muslim teens to "at-risk gangbangers, who want to stand up for their community, to address grievances of the global Muslim community more effectively than they've seen the elder generation."

Elibiary has defended Sayyid Qutb, the Islamist ideologue credited with inspiring the Muslim Brotherhood and terrorist groups including al-Qaida. He recommends Qutb's writing as offering "the potential for a strong spiritual rebirth that's truly ecumenical allowing all faiths practiced in America to enrich us and motivate us to serve God better by serving our fellow man more."

Rashad Hussain – Special Envoy to the (OIC) Organization of the Islamic Conference. A Global Muslim Brotherhood Daily Report took a look at Hussain's official biography and found several concerning affiliations. The first is that in October 2000, Hussain spoke at a conference sponsored by the Association of Muslim Social Scientists, which was listed in an internal Muslim Brotherhood document as one of "our organizations and the organizations of our friends," and the Prince Alwaleed Center for Muslim-Christian Understanding of Georgetown University, which receives Saudi funding and is directed by prominent Muslim Brotherhood advocate, John Esposito.

In September 2004, Hussain played a role in the Muslim Students Association's annual conference, which was founded by Muslim Brotherhood in 1963 and is also listed as one the group's fronts in its own documents. Since then, many of its nearly 600 college chapters have engaged in extremism and the group closely collaborates with the other Brotherhood fronts. For example, MSA was part of an umbrella organization called the American Muslim Taskforce that led a campaign against the FBI's use of informants in mosques and accused the agency of anti-Muslim activity. Several Brotherhood affiliates are in this including the Muslim-American Society, the Islamic Circle of North America, the Islamic Society of North America, the Muslim Public Affairs Council and the Council on American-Islamic Relations.

At this conference, Hussain spoke alongside the daughter of Professor Sami Al-Arian, who was convicted of being a key leader of the Palestinian Islamic Jihad terrorist group and later admitted to being a member of the Muslim Brotherhood. Hussain also defended Al-Arian and described his prosecution as being a "politically-motivated persecution."

The network of Brotherhood-affiliated groups has consistently been on his side throughout the entire ordeal and celebrated his release. Interestingly, the story in The Washington Report on Middle East Affairs that quoted Hussain's defense of Al-Arian has been altered since its original publication. A cnsnews article reports that the quote was removed "sometime after October 2007" and that the reporter who wrote the article expressed surprise but said she no longer worked at WRMEA and could not explain the edit.

Last May, Hussain spoke at a conference sponsored by several Brotherhood affiliates, including the Muslim Public Affairs Council, an organization whose extremism has been catalogued in a A series by The Investigative Project on Terrorism and the Council on American-Islamic Relations. The latter was listed by the federal government in 2007 as an 'unindicted co-conspirator' in the terrorism financing trial of The Holy Land Foundation, another Muslim Brotherhood front that was found to be financing Hamas. Its founders are former officials at the Islamic Association of Palestine, a Brotherhood front shut down for supporting Hamas and are said by the FBI to be members of the Brotherhood's Palestine Committee in the United States.

Hussain's view on the cause of terrorism is important to note as it will play a significant role in the Obama Administration's outreach to the Muslim world. He quoted a study that concluded that 'The primary cause of broad-based anger and anti-Americanism is not a clash of civilizations but the perceived effect of U.S. foreign policy in the Muslim world.' In this statement, it appears that he believes that terrorism is the product of opposition to foreign policy, rather than the product of a politico-religious totalitarian ideology, which explains his opposition to terms like "Islamic terrorism."

On the other hand, Hussein does support the use of the term "Hamas terrorists," so he cannot be said to be a supporter of Hamas, which grew out of the Muslim Brotherhood. He has an entire section in his paper titled, 'Discrediting the Terrorist Ideology.' He opposes making democracy promotion a central part of that goal, saying that it can be interpreted as imperialism and an attempt to bring about freedom that enables immorality, but admits that it may be part of the solution. He instead suggests that the government use Muslim voices to argue that Islam forbids acts of terrorism and extremism.

One other important part of his paper is when he proposes that the U.S. build a Muslim coalition "not limited to those who advocate Western-style democracy, and avoid creating a dichotomy between freedom and Islamic society." This would set the stage for a partnership with the Muslim Brotherhood. Rather than focusing on supporting elements that will genuinely argue that democracy is compatible with Islam, his standard for allies is that they just oppose terrorism and extremism. Apparently, those who pursue Sharia Law through other methods do not fit his version of 'extremist.'

Salam al-Marayati – Obama Adviser, founder of Muslim Public Affairs Council and its current executive director. This is an article by the Militant Islam Monitor, on May 11, 2013, regarding al-Marayati:

"Salam Al Marayati, the director of the Muslim Public Affairs Council (MPAC), is scheduled to be on a panel at the upcoming National Homeland Security Conference in June in LA. The panel discussion is about "Public and Private" Partnerships. The program tracks "Interoperability, Information Sharing and Intelligence."

Arif Alikhan ,who was responsible for derailing the LAPD's plans to monitor activities within the Muslim community is also a speaker at the conference, He was appointed as assistant secretary for the Office of Policy Development in Barack Obama's Department of Homeland Security in 2009. According to 'Discover the Networks': MPAC has defended the use of terrorism and Al Marayati said on the radio on 9/11 that Israel could have been behind the attacks." In a November 1997 speech at the University of Pennsylvania, MPAC Co-Founder and Executive Director Salam Al-Marayati steadfastly refused to call Hezbollah a terrorist organization; he justified the existence of Hamas as a political entity and a provider of social programs and "educational operations" and he equated jihad with the sentiments of the American statesman Patrick Henry, whose "Give me liberty or give me death" declaration was, in Al-Marayati's view, "a way of looking at the term 'jihad' from an American perspective."

Al-Marayati will be participating in the NHS conference under the aegis of the Muslim American Homeland Security Congress an Islamist organization which attempts to prevent law enforcement scrutiny of Muslims, deny any Islamic connection to terrorism and hinder government efforts to educate people about the jihadist threat. Among the MAHSC listed board members is the Council on American Islamic Relations (CAIR) a Saudi funded front group for Hamas and an unindicted co-conspirator in the Holyland Foundation Hamas funding trial.

It should come as no surprise that Haroon Azar,the DHS Security Regional Director for Strategic Engagement, has worked with MPAC in the past. Haroon Azar took part in an MPAC teleconference aimed at portraying Muslims as victims of a non existent backlash after the Boston terrorist attacks. Azar is also speaking on the same panel as Al Marayati at the upcoming NHS conference.

To have a documented Islamist leader of a major Muslim organization with known terrorist sympathies and Muslim Brotherhood ties on a panel at a NHS conference is further proof that our security apparatus is being manipulated by and adopting a jihadist perspective while doing everything it can to deny and obscure the threat which radical Islam poses to the security of the United States.

Imam Mohamed Magid – Obama's Sharia Czar, Islamic Society of North America. A PJ Media report on July 5, 2012 gave the following information about Mohamed Magid and his support for other radical Islamists:

"Mohamed Magid is the Obama administration's go-to guy for Muslim outreach and advise on international affairs and counterterrorism. He is a regular visitor to the White House (even when the administration wants to conceal it,) attends important administration speeches on the US Middle East policy at the State Department, he counsels the Department of Justice to criminalize defamation of Islam, he entertains the deputy national security adviser at his DC-area mosque, and he serves on the Department of Homeland Security's Countering Violent Extremism Working Group. He also advises the FBI and many other federal agencies. He has also been profiled by Time Magazine and the Huffington Post has even dubbed him "America's Imam." His ubiquitous presence across the Obama administration undoubtedly makes him the most influential and sought after Muslim authority in the country.

Imam Magid also serves as the president of the Islamic Society of North America (ISNA). In that capacity last weekend he presided over ISNA's "Diversity Forum" held in Dearborn (where Muslim residents were recently video recorded stoning Christian protestors). One of the speakers at the ISNA Diversity Forum was CAIR-Michigan executive director Dawud Walid. Imam Magid even gave a "diversity award" to Walid.

Walid, too, is popular with the Obama administration, taking two taxpayer financed trips overseas on behalf of the State Department. But just a little over a month ago Dawud Walid gave a sermon at the Islamic Organization of America (IONA) mosque in Warren, Michigan. As noted by an Investigative Project report issued just days after Walid's appearance, during the sermon he asked, "Who are those who incurred the wrath of Allah?" Answering his own question in Arabic, he replied, "They are the Jews, they are the

Islamization

Will Clark

Jews." Walid also took aim his imagined enemies, saying:

"One of the greatest social ills facing American today is Islamophobia, and anti-Muslim bigotry. And if you trace the organizations and the main advocates and activists in Islamophobia in America, you will see that all those organizations are pro-Israeli occupation organizations and activists."

So not only are the Jews the cursed of Allah, but the Jews are also behind "Islamophobia" — reviving longtime Islamic blood libels. As the Investigative Project report goes on to note Walid has also taken to Twitter to correctly source and affirm Islamic authorities who called for killing Jews.

Imam Magid's endorsement of Walid's outspoken Jew-hatred raises some serious questions about who Obama is getting his advice from, but it does answer some questions about the inspiration for the Obama administration's ongoing "Islamophobia" witchhunt. But handing a "diversity award" to an unashamed Jew-hater doesn't make Dawud Walid a diversity hero. It does, however, say something about Obama's Shariah czar Mohamed Magid."

Eboo Patel – Advisory Council on Faith-Based Neighborhood Partnerships. Named by US News & World Report as one of America's Best Leaders of 2009, Eboo Patel is the founder and Executive Director of Interfaith Youth Core (IFYC), a Chicago-based institution building the global interfaith youth movement. Author of the award-winning book 'Acts of Faith: The Story of an American Muslim, the Struggle for the Soul of a Generation,' Eboo is also a regular contributor to the Washington Post,

National Public Radio and CNN. He is a member of President Obama's Advisory Council of the White House Office of Faith Based and Neighborhood Partnerships, and holds a doctorate in the sociology of religion from Oxford University, where he studied on a Rhodes scholarship.

Although nothing specific has been reported to suggest he has the same Islamic inclinations as the others reported above, his inclusion in Obama's close administration must still be suspect. The idea of a 'global interfaith youth movement' itself could be suspect considering all the other aspects of Islam. Their ultimate goal is to turn everyone into Islamists. And, combine this approach with the global internet connection with all schools - they have the perfect vehicle to begin that insidious project.

Supporting ISNA

Barack Obama and his administration have supported and promoted many of these Islamists under the guise of peace building and inclusion. But is that what's really happening? Let's analyze just one organization they openly support - ISNA: The Islamic Society of North America. According to The Investigative Project on Terrorism, ISNA is probably the most dangerous organization to our existence as Americans. Their investigation gives more information:

"Established in 1981 by the Saudi-funded Muslim Students' Association of the U.S. and Canada (MSA), the Islamic Society of North America (ISNA) calls itself the largest Muslim organization on the continent. ISNA was created by MSA with the help of one of Palestanian Islamic Jihad's founding students, Sami Al-Irian. Another noteworthy founding member of ISNA was Mahboob Khan.

Today ISNA's annual conventions draw more attendees, usually over 30,000, more than any other Muslim gathering in the western hemisphere. ISNA's mission is to function as "an association of Muslim organizations and individuals that provides a common platform for presenting Islam, supporting Muslim communities, developing educational, social and outreach programs and fostering good relations with other religious communities, and civic and service organizations."

ISNA focuses heavily on providing Wahhabi theological indoctrination materials to a large percentage of the mosques in North America. Many of these mosques were recently built with Saudi money and are required, by their Saudi benefactors, to strictly follow the dictates of Wahhabi imams; an edict that affects the tone and content of the sermons given in the mosques, the selection of books and periodicals that may be read in mosque libraries or sold in mosque bookshops, and the policies governing the exclusion or suppression of dissenters from the congregations.

Through its affiliate, the North American Islamic Trust, a Saudi government-backed organization created to fund Islamist enterprises in North America, the Saudi-subsidized ISNA reportedly holds the mortgages on 50 to 80 percent of all mosques in the U.S. and Canada. Thus the organization can freely exercise ultimate authority over these houses of worship and their teachings.

Writes Kaukab Siddique, the editor of 'New Trend,' an Islamic periodical of extremist views that is nonetheless opposed to Wahhabi domination of American Islam: "ISNA controls most mosques in America and thus also controls who will speak at every Friday prayer, and which literature will be distributed there."

Islam scholar Stephen Schwartz describes ISNA as "one of the chief conduits through which the radical Saudi form of Islam passes into the United States."Adds Schwartz, "Our view is that the number of mosques under Wahhabi control actually totals at least 600 out of the official total of 1,200, while, as noted, Shia community leaders endorse the figure of 80 percent Wahhabi control. But we also offer a number of 6,000 mosques overall, including small and diverse congregations of many kinds."

According to Sufi leader Sheikh Muhammad Hisham Kabbani's testimony before a State Department Open Forum on January 7, 1999, extremists have taken over "more than 80 percent of the mosques in the United States. This means that the ideology of extremism has been spread to 80 percent of the Muslim population, mostly the youth and the new generation." Kabbani based his statement on his personal investigation of 114 American mosques. "Ninety of them," he said, "were mostly exposed, and I say exposed, to extreme or radical ideology, based on their speeches, books and board members." This is largely due to the efforts of ISNA.

According to terrorism expert Steven Emerson, ISNA "is a radical group hiding under a false veneer of moderation;" "convenes annual conferences where Islamist militants have been given a platform to incite violence and promote hatred" (for instance, al Qaeda supporter and PLO official Yusuf Al-Qaradhawi was invited to speak at an ISNA conference); has held fundraisers for terrorists (after Hamas leader Mousa Marzook was arrested and eventually deported in 1997, ISNA raised money for his defense); has condemned the U.S. government's post-9/11 seizure of Hamas' and Palestinian Islamic Jihad's financial assets; and publishes a bi-monthly magazine, '*Islamic Horizons*,' that "often champions militant Islamist doctrine." End of article.

Many more Islamic organizations, almost all in fact, that are aimed at the one goal of a silent Jihad of changing America to Sharia from within. They have all assigned themselves to that charter - and Barack Obama is helping them achieve that goal.

The hard truth is: they could not accomplish that Jihadist goal without Obama's help. Is he helping them destroy the United States from sheer stupidity, or is he really part of that Jihad, himself? Perhaps he really does understand what he's doing. Or, is he perhaps guided in his relationship with Muslim terrorists by a statement he made in 2007?

On November 21, 2007, then-candidate Obama said on New Hampshire Public Radio that his Muslim experience would make us safer:

"I truly believe that the day I'm inaugurated, not only the country looks at itself differently, but the world looks at America differently. If I'm reaching out to the Muslim world they understand that I've lived in a Muslim country and I may be a Christian, but I also understand their point of view.

My sister is half-Indonesian. I traveled there all the way through my college years. And so I'm intimately concerned with what happens in these countries and the cultures and perspective these folks have. And those are powerful tools for us to be able to reach out to the world. Then I think the world will have confidence that I am listening to them and that our future and our security is tied up with our ability to work with other countries in the world that will ultimately make us safer."

Is Obama delusional, or is he lost in la-la land? The radical Muslim terrorist goal is to destroy us and anyone else who is not or does not convert to Islam. Why does he think his relationship with them, or who he is, will change that dogma? It seems his policies are leaned more to helping the silent jihad infiltrate into our schools, as well as everywhere else, instead of establishing policies to help our school educate our children and help them find a sense of self worth, so they might find personal success, that will help the economy of America, as well as helping them find happiness for themselves.

Education Encroachment

This post at islaminourschools.com on Nov 20, 2014 lists several articles that help identify the Muslim Brotherhood's encroachment into our schools to implement their long range plan of transforming America into a Muslim nation. This focus on schools is only one part of their plan for consuming the United States by the 'Settlement' concept explained earlier in this book This compilation of articles is titled: 'Islam In Our Schools.'

Title: 'Marine Dad banned from school files lawsuit for Islamic indoctrination.' Posted on November 20, 2014 by careylj. The original article was posted at Charisma News by Catherine Mcmillan:

The Thomas More Law Center (TMLC) today announced its representation of John Kevin Wood, and his wife, Melissa, in their battle with La Plata High School in Maryland over the Islamic indoctrination of their 11th-grade daughter in her World History class. Their daughter was required to complete assignments where she had to affirm that "There is no god but Allah" and the other Five Pillars of Islam.

The case gained national attention when the school banned John Wood from entering school property after he objected to the religion of Islam being taught in his daughter's history class and demanded that she be given an alternative assignment. The school refused.

Wood, a former Marine who served in Operation Desert Shield/Desert Storm and lost friends in that action, saw first hand the destruction caused in the name of Allah and that Islam is not "a religion of peace;" and he would not budge from his position.

The Thomas More Law Center is a national public-interest law firm based in Ann Arbor, Michigan. TMLC Senior Trial Counsel, Erin Mersino, and Maryland attorney, Michael F. Smith of The Smith Appellate Law Firm, represent the Wood family. Yesterday they filed a request for records relating to the case under Maryland's Public Information Act.

On Oct. 22, 2014, John Wood discovered that his daughter was being forced to repeat religious tenets of Islam as a part of her World History class assignment. She was required to write how the prophet Muhammad was visited by the angel Gabriel and preached that there is only one true god, who is Allah. The assignment made her write that Mohammad is the messenger of Allah and that the Quran is holy text.

The assignment required her to affirm that "Allah is the same god that is worshipped in Christianity and Judaism" and that the "Quran is the word of Allah revealed to Mohammad in the same way that Jews and Christians believe the Torah and the Gospels were revealed to Moses and the New Testament writers." The assignment also forced young women such as the Woods' daughter, to fill in the following sentences: "Men are the managers of the affairs of women" and "Righteous women are therefore obedient."

When John Wood discovered the Islamic propaganda and indoctrination, he was rightfully outraged, and that evening unsuccessfully tried to contact the school by phone to voice his objections. Wood witnessed firsthand the destruction caused in the name of Allah and knows Islam is not "a religion of peace." He served in Operation Desert Shield/Desert Storm, and lost friends in that action. On 9-11, Wood responded as a firefighter to the smoldering Pentagon. He refused to allow La Plata High School to subject his daughter to Islamic indoctrination despite the threatened academic consequences.

The next day, Oct. 23, Wood had a phone conversation with a La Plata vice principal where he again reiterated his objections to his daughter being indoctrinated into the religion of Islam. The vice principal indicated that his daughter, a high school junior with college hopes, would receive zeros on her assignments on Islam if she did not complete them. He asked how the religion of Islam could be taught when schools are prohibited from teaching the religion of Christianity.

The following day, Oct. 24, John Wood again spoke with the vice principal. She again refused to allow an alternative assignment.

Commenting on the case, Richard Thompson, TMLC's President and Chief Counsel stated: "Adding insult to injury, in an arrogant and unnecessary display of power, La Plata's principal issued a written "No Trespass" notice, which denied this former Marine who stood in harm's way defending our country—which included the principal and her staff—any access to school grounds. The school's actions not only dishonored John Wood's service, but the service of all men and women in our Armed Forces who defended our nation from Islamic violence. True to his Marine training, John Wood stood his ground. He did not retreat. Yes, his daughter has received a failing grade in her World History Class. But the story is not yet over."

Title: 'NC School misrepresents Islam, caught red handed by mom.' Posted on November 14, 2014 by careylj:

A teacher at Porter Ridge High School in Indian Trail, NC came under fire this week after a mother reviewed her son's homework assignment. Like many schools around the nation, this one was studying Islam as part of the state approved curriculum, although none of the sources covering this story identified the publisher and title of the text being used. Nevertheless, the worksheet given to students has several troubling statements. Also note, the school has not confirmed if the answers written by this student are the correct answers based on class content, but there is little reason to believe otherwise. (A picture of the handout is shown in the original article.)

1. The handout suggests "Islam is the fastest growing religion in the world". On the face of it, this is correct. But what is left unsaid is more informative and important. It is very troubling this statement is made without qualifiers. Islam is fastest growing only in terms of reproduction among Muslim families. Muslim women are having more babies than non-Muslim women, and all children are deemed to be Muslim per sharia. Unlike Christianity, where a child is not a Christian until he or she makes that choice personally, all children in Islamic households do not get a choice; they are already assumed to be Muslim. But in terms of conversion rates, Islam certainly is NOT the fastest growing religion in the world. The statement is loaded and may be intended to suggest that since Islam is the fastest growing religion, there must be an intellectual reason – Islam must be intellectually appealing for others to be drawn to it in record numbers. Such is NOT the case.

2. "Experts predict it will be the largest religion in the world some

day." Again, very misleading and suggestive that Islam has an intellectual appeal drawing record numbers into its fold. Such is not the case. And who exactly are the 'experts' being cited? What is the source of the criteria used? How was the research conducted? These questions may have been introduced in the classroom, but we have legitimate reasons to ask these tough questions, especially when it concerns intellectual honesty and integrity.

3. "Islam is, at heart, a peaceful religion." This is patently false. There are two reasons why this statement would be made. Either the one making the claim has not studied Islam for herself, or she is deliberately attempting to portray Islam in a positive manner for other purposes to cover its true doctrine and make it palatable to Western sensitivities. Although there are peaceful Muslims, there is no peaceful Islam. The Quran is replete with scripture commanding Muslims to slaughter, mutilate, and behead all non-Muslims without limitations on time, place, or circumstance. Muhammad, whom Muslims believe to be the perfect example of righteous conduct (Quran 33:21) commanded the slaughter of those who mocked him, wrote poetry criticizing him, or opposed his claim to be God's final prophet. These are all documented in the earliest and most authoritative biography of Muhammad's life, written by Ibn Ishaq a mere 130 years after Muhammad's death. I have highlighted some of these incidents in this article. Ibn Ishaq's biography of Muhammad is the standard text all scholars of Islam use when studying his life, and it paints a picture of the man starkly different than the statement on the student worksheet. Statements that Islam is peaceful fly in the face of historical reality of 1,400 years of Islamic aggression and do not align at all with the example Muhammad set for his followers.

4. "Most Muslims [sic] faith is stronger than the average Christian." This seems to be opinion offered as fact, a common

tactic found when teaching Islam around the nation. On what research is this opinion based? Again, such a statement seems to have one purpose in mind: to elevate Islam as superior to any other religion. This is indoctrination, not education.

5. "Radical Islamic fundamentalists are opposed to Western Civilization's way of life and imperialistic pursuits." Again, a fundamentally incorrect view of the historical reality. Radical Islamic fundamentalism began just a few short years after the death of Muhammad, and centuries before any Western power began imperialistic pursuits. In fact, scholar Efraim Karsh has documented such Islamic imperialism in his book, aptly titled "Islamic Imperialism: A History." Another excellent resource, researched with abundant citations, is Andrew Bostom's "The Legacy of Jihad." Western society, foreign policy, and other arguments are nothing more than a smokescreen to hide 1,400 years of Islamic aggression sanctioned by Islam's holy text and Muhammad's commands.

6. "These fundamentalists represent a small percentage of the population of Islam ..." Two comments here. 1) Estimates put the number of so-called extremist fundamentalists at around twenty percent. Although one might call this a small percentage, twenty percent of 1.8 billion still represents 360 million, larger than the population of the United States. Is this really a small number and of no concern? 2) Although the news media prefer to focus on the actions of extremist groups like Boko Haram, Al Qaeda, or the Islamic State, much of the persecution and terrorism against non-Muslims is at the hands of normal, every day, ordinary Muslims, not these extremist groups. The twenty percent number thus is an under estimate of the number of Muslims involved in what would be considered terrorism against non-Muslims. Consider, for example, the Arab Spring riots in Egypt not long ago. Churches were burned, Christians driven from their homes, their businesses

looted and burned, not at the hands of extremists, but regular Muslims. The same can be said of countless other similar events across the globe.

7. "No where [sic] in the Qur'an does it say you will go to paradise if you martyr yourself with a suicide bomb." On the face of it, this is a correct statement but misleading. The Qur'an never uses the word 'bomb' anywhere. But both the Qur'an and the hadith (traditions attributed to Muhammad) speak extensively of those who sacrifice their lives as martyrs in the service of Islam. Sahih Bukhari, the second most authoritative set of texts for Sunni Muslims after the Qur'an, dedicates an entire 50 or so page section on jihad. The blessings of martyrdom are given ample attention. Further, the Qur'an speaks directly to this topic in Sura 3:169-170, which says, "Think not of those who are killed in the Way of Allâh as dead. Nay, they are alive, with their Lord, and they have provision. They rejoice in what Allâh has bestowed upon them of His Bounty, rejoicing for the sake of those who have not yet joined them, but are left behind (not yet martyred) that on them no fear shall come, nor shall they grieve."

8. "To win (the war on terror) we need to raise the standard of living in areas of squalor and educate so as to avoid political brainwashing." The war on terror, and terrorism itself, has absolutely nothing to do with uneducated Muslims living poverty. This is one point drive home time and again by liberals and leftists who think poverty is the driving force behind Islamic militant movements. But consider these simple facts that will put to rest this notion. 1) Osama bin Laden, perhaps the best known terrorist, was both well educated and a multi-millionaire. 2) A significant percentage of young Muslim men joining ranks with militant Islamic movements come from wealthy households and are college graduates, some with advanced degrees. 3) If poverty drives extremism, why do we not see people living in poverty in other

cultures forming militant groups and forcing their brand of religion upon the rest of the world?

The version of Islam being presented in our schools today is nothing short of brain washing and indoctrination. It has been this way for several years, but finally others are beginning to take notice. Parents must be vigilant to know what their child is being taught, and speak out when errors like these are noticed. We the people have the power to make a difference. To see how one group of common citizens is taking on this issue in Texas, visit the website of TruthInTexasTextbooks.

Title: 'The Mosqueing of Public Schools in America.' Posted on November 13, 2014 by careylj. Originally posted by Pamela Geller:

I have been fielding calls from distraught parents all week, reeling from the proselytizing for Islam in their children's "social studies" or "world history" classes. They are not teaching the children "world history," which would include Islam's 1,400-year history of jihadi wars, land appropriations, cultural annihilations and enslavements, not to mention the extermination of the entire Jewish Banu Qurayza tribe of Arabia.

Instead, children are forced to recite the Shahada. (It's an Islamic creed one says to convert to Islam.) Instead, they are forced to learn the five pillars of Islam.

This is an outrage, but expected and exactly what I warned of in my book, "Stop the Islamization of America: A Practical Guide to the Resistance," in the chapter, "The Mosqueing of the Public Schools."

One mother with whom I spoke told me that her 12-year-old son came home from school "depressed" and "sick." Coming from a "good Christian home," he was confused and "hurt" that he had to write and say the Muslim declaration of faith (the Shahada), and write it repeatedly. The mother was beside herself.

Title: 'Massachusetts school curriculum upsets parents.' Posted on October 30, 2014 by careylj:

Parents in Revere, Massachusetts are understandably upset over the way Islam is being taught during a course in history. Some parents in Revere were angry when they learned students were being taught about Islam and the Muslim religion.

"No religion should be taught at school. In their paper it says Allah is their only God. That's insulting to me as a Christian who believes in just Jesus only," said Anthony Giannino.

A section of the textbook describing the beliefs of Muslims says, "I bear witness that there is no God but Allah."

Giannino immediately pulled his son out of the classroom. "We don't believe in Allah. I don't believe in my son learning about this here," he said. "If my son was from another country and came here, he would have been catered to. But where he's not being catered to, they give him an F."

History is no doubt a subject for academic pursuit, and no history lesson would be complete without mention of the various religious belief systems that have shaped history around the world. But when the subject matter deviates from history to theology, it crosses the line. In Massachusetts, the textbook being used deviates into indoctrination, as do many texts around the country. The text declared there is no God but Allah, and that Muhammad is the messenger of Allah, the first step to becoming a Muslim.

Herein is the danger: This phrase is known as the shahada, the Islamic confession of faith, by which one officially becomes a Muslim upon uttering the confession. School children, unbeknown to them, have confessed to be a Muslim simply by having their teacher recite the shahada aloud in class as part of a history or cultural studies program.

I wonder if Christianity is given the same treatment with the teacher having the students repeat the sinner's prayer with her/him.

The problem is compounded by the fact that major textbook publishers have Muslim scholars on their editorial boards. This in itself should not be problematic, for who knows better about Islam than a Muslim scholar. The problem arises when such scholars go to great lengths to distort or gloss over the rather unsavory aspects of Islam's past, Muhammad's behavior, and a great number of verses in the Quran which paint Islam as a supremacist ideology bent on subjecting the world to it's ideology. Such editorial boards have such a naive understanding of Islam, they will believe anything their Islamic representative tells them. This is not only unfortunate, but dangerous.

Mark Durie puts it well why non-Muslims must study Islam for themselves and not rely on Islamic scholars to tell us what they want us to know about Islam, all the while hiding the less palatable aspects of Islam. From his book "The Third Choice: Islam, Dhimmitude, and Freedom"

Misinformation about Islam is a constant issue for non-Muslims. A report in the Herald Sun, a major Melbourne daily newspaper, was published on August 8, 2005 stating that the senior Muslim Imam of Victoria, Sheikh Fehmi (subsequently appointed as Australia's mufti) reassured non-Muslims in Victoria that Muslims wish only to live in peace with their non-Muslim neighbours:

'Muslims live cheerfully and happily with all denominations,' Sheik Fehmi said. 'This is what Islam is. The Prophet has lived among Jews and Christians. In many parts of the world Muslims, Jews and Christians are living happily.'

Who would not applaud Sheikh Fehmi's desire for people of different faiths to live together in harmony? The problem arises when he appeals to Muhammad's example as the basis for non-Muslims to have confidence, that Muslim neighbours represent no threat to peaceful co-existence. Although there was a time when Muhammad lived peacefully alongside non Muslims, large sections of Muhammad's biographies deal with periods when he was embattled with his non-Muslim Jewish neighbours. Muhammad ordered assassinations of women and old men, oversaw a mass decapitation and enslavement of hundreds of his Jewish neighbours. This darker material Sheikh Fehmi could not fail to be familiar with, as these victories of Islam over the Jews of Arabia are as well-known to Muslim children as Joshua's conquest of Jericho has been to Sunday School children.

How then are Fehmi's non-Muslim, fellow Victorians to understand what he means by his reassurances that they can have nothing to worry about, because Islam takes Muhammad as its example? Should non-Muslims just regard this as propaganda, or is it to be understood as a threat?

If a non-Muslim were to have written in response to Sheikh Fehmi's comment in the Herald Sun, pointing out Muhammad's less than happy relationships with his non-Muslim neighbours, how could this be done without sounding like incitement of interfaith conflict and a rejection of Fehmi's apparently moderate and peaceful stance? By relying on acceptance of the excellence of Muhammad's example as a condition of interfaith harmony, Sheikh Fehmi's words serve to lock up the truth about Muhammad even more tightly in the dark box of ignorance.

These are not easy subjects to deal with, but deal with them we must, and one of the keys to a free and frank conversation with Muslims about such matters of importance is that non-Muslims must study Islam for themselves. They cannot rely on Muslim spokespeople as their only source of information on Islam. The same can be said for Muslims: they also should not rely on secondary sources, not even on Islamic clerics, to understand their faith.

Title: 'Hundreds will protest Islam lovefest history textbook foisted on high school students.' Posted on November 5, 2013 by careylj:

On Florida's Atlantic Coast, some 200 or more local parents and activists have announced plans to show up at Tuesday's Volusia County school board meeting to protest the public school use of a world history textbook that devotes a whole chapter to Islam but exactly zero chapters to any other religions.

The textbook, called simply "World History," contains a 32-page chapter fondly devoted to "Muslim Civilizations." Sections include descriptions of the Koran, the growth of the Muslim empire and the Five Pillars of Islam.

The planned protest will include a demand that students rip out the 32 pages of the Islam chapter unless the school district agrees to provide students with a similar amount of officially-sanctioned material concerning other religions, reports local ABC affiliate WFTV, which adds:

"The seeds for the Wednesday protest were reportedly planted after an unidentified local mother started a Facebook page demanding that local, taxpayer-funded schools stop using the textbook. The district indicated that it will continue to use the controversial book.

School district officials in Volusia County insist that there's no problem because other religions come up as a matter of course in the book. Thus, the argument goes, there's no need to have a single chapter dedicated to, say, the Gospels or the Pentateuch—or, for that matter, Hindu or Buddhist religious traditions.

"Christianity and Judaism is [sic] spread throughout the book," a school district spokeswoman told WFTV.

The book's supporters also argue that students know about Christianity but need to learn more about Islam because of its crucial importance in international affairs.

On Monday, the Council on American-Islamic Relations (CAIR) issued a statement criticizing the protesters.

"This group is displaying an alarming level of intolerance and brazen disregard of minority religions here in the US. We find their actions Un-American and against every core principal that makes this country so great," CAIR said.

Critics of the textbook include District 2 Deltona commissioner Webster Barnaby, who told WFTV that he is only seeking equal time for other religions, specifically Christianity. "The problem is: there needs to be balance. In America today, Christianity is being relegated to the trash heap," Barnaby told the station. "Why relegate Christianity to a footnote in an entire history book, and you give an entire chapter on the teachings of Islam?" he added.

"To suggest that everybody knows about Christianity, that is total ignorance," Barnaby also said.

The "World History" textbook is one of three textbooks covering similar material that meet Florida's criteria for adoption by the state's public schools.

As a school district spokeswoman noted, one reason school districts select this book is because it covers information required under Florida's Next Generation Sunshine State Standards—the state's version of the Common Core.

The same textbook is used in school districts across Florida and across the country. Certainly, the book is no stranger to debate in Florida. There has already been at least one dust-up — in Brevard County — a few months ago.

Title: 'Tennessee HS students get copy of Quran at mosque field trip.' Posted on September 18, 2013 by careylj:

A Tennessee high school has decided to revise its field trip policy after a group of freshmen were taken to an Islamic mosque where they were given copies of the Koran and while a student who opted out of the trip was given a worksheet that alleged Muslims treated their conquered people better than the United States treated minorities.

The students were in an honors world studies class at Hendersonville High School and the field trips to the mosque as well as a Hindu temple were part of a three-week course on world religions.

But some parents objected to the trips and wondered why the school would tour a mosque but not a Christian church or a Jewish synagogue.

"If you can't go to all five, why are you going to any?" asked parent Mike Conner. "We sent the principal an email and voiced our concerns. She sent back a reply and told us they could not afford to go to all five."

Children were given punch and cookies at the mosque where they listened to readings from the Koran, Conner said. They were also given copies of the Islamic holy book – which some students took and others declined.

During their visit to the Hindu temple, students engaged in meditation.

"Our kids are being indoctrinated and this is being shoved in their face," Conner told Fox News. "It tells me they are pushing other religions and they want Christianity to take a back seat. They want our children to be tolerant of everything except Christianity."

Title: 'Florida State Rep: History Textbook an Islam love fest.' Posted on August 4, 2013 by careylj. From The Daily Caller:

A Florida school board is reviewing a state-approved world history textbook used in an Advanced Placement class over claims that the book covers Islam in loving, rah-rah detail while giving short shrift to Christianity and Judaism.

The textbook – called simply World History – is published under Pearson's Prentice Hall imprint and is currently in use in an A.P. class in Brevard County schools—and in school districts across the country.

It contains a 36-page chapter fondly devoted to "Muslim

Civilizations," reports FOX News. Sections include discussions of the rise of Islam and the growth of the Muslim empire.

Take a wild guess about the number of chapters the book dedicates to Christianity or Judaism. That's right: zero.

"It's remarkably one-sided," said Ritch Workman, a Republican member of the Florida House of Representatives who raised the ruckus that started the review process.

Title: 'Florida history textbook under fire. 'Posted on August 2, 2013 by careylj, Prentice Hall World History:

Yet another so-called history textbook is under fire, this time in Florida. And like other similar cases around the country, this textbook teaches a revisionist and sugar-coated view of Islam and devotes much more coverage to Islam than any other world religion.

Todd Starnes of Fox News reports in this article one glaring example of a sugar-coated revisionist history stated as fact in this book. The book says, "Jihad may be interpreted as a holy war to defend Islam and the Muslim community, much like the Crusades to defend Christianity." At best, this statement is misleading and incomplete, and at worst it is inaccurate and wrong. One should expect students in our public schools to receive accurate and truthful information, particularly when studying history.

Title: 'Tennessee parents angry after school textbooks justify Palestinian suicide bombings.' Posted on April 30, 2013 by Joe:

Tennessee parents are fuming after learning that school textbooks justify Palestinian suicide bombings in Israel. Some parents in Williamson County, Tennessee, are calling for the removal of the high school textbook, believing that it is biased against Israel.

The textbook is taught on a college level elective course called Human Geography, and is available to students in public schools in Williamson County, which also offer an elective course on the Bible.

Parents are against the kind of questions that the book is encouraging teens to ask. One of the book's questions is: "If a Palestinian suicide bomber kills dozens of Israeli teenagers in a restaurant in Jerusalem, is it an act of terrorism or a war against the policies of the Israeli government?"

Julie West, a mother of a 15-year-old student at Franklin High School in Franklin, Tennessee, said the question is pro-Palestinian.

"We are living in a time where people say: 'How can someone put a bomb outside a restaurant or on a street with the intention of killing innocent people?' And we wonder why, when at the same time we are teaching our children a curriculum that suggests it could be fine, or at least it might be okay if these children are Jewish," West said.

Laurie Cardoza-Moore, head of a pro Israeli group, said: "the book is anti-Semitic." Cardoza-Moore said that the book aims to delegitimize the right of the Jewish people to the Holy Land.

"I am shocked that such a book even exists in the U.S. It should be illegal. What is it doing in a school in Tennessee? This book seems more fitting for some radical country located thousands of miles away from the U.S." Jerold Peralta, of Scottsdale, Arizona told YourJewishNews.com after learning about the book.

"I think it's a slippery slope to go down if we start banning books, because people have opposing views," county schools Superintendent Mike Looney said. "I think the fundamental question to be answered is: Does the book create an opportunity for students to engage in deep dialogue about important issues in the world? I think it does," Looney added.

One response to this article was: "Far too many in our nation are still under the illusion, as is the instructor mentioned in this article, that the cause of Arab and/or Palestinian hatred of Jews is somehow rooted in Israeli or United States foreign policy issues. They refuse to recognize that Islamic jihad has been a reality on the historical scene for long before Israel or the United States even existed. Nor do they wish to recognize hatred of Jews has theological roots embedded in Islamic teaching.

Let me quote just a small snippet as an example of the theological roots of hatred against Jews from Muslims. Kate McCord wrote her book "In The Land of Blue Burqas" to tell of her experience of living for five years among common, ordinary Afghanis. In her book, she relates the following:

'An Afghan man, a graduate of Sharia law school, explained what he called the correct Islamic perspective on Israel. He said that the Jews have disobeyed God and are forever beyond redemption. That means, even if they convert to Islam, they still cannot be saved. He said that God hates the Jews and will never forgive them. He said that God has ordered the nation of Islam, the entire worldwide community of Muslims, to annihilate the Jews.'

Does this sound like Jew hatred is caused by Israeli foreign policy issues?

Title: Texas students told to wear burkas. Posted on March 29, 2013 by careylj:

There's a new controversy in Texas involving the online public school curriculum called CSCOPE, which already has been the subject of heated debate and state legislative hearings.

There are reports now that students were made to wear Muslim burqas as part of their public school lessons.

CSCOPE has been facing criticism over its alleged Islamic and anti-American bias. It is a "curriculum management system" now used in 80 percent of Texas classrooms. It recently was the subject of a heated inquiry that culminated in hearings conducted by the Texas Senate Education Committee chaired by state Sen. Dan Patrick, R-Houston.

Texas Curriculum: Allah is Almighty God! Posted on December 15, 2012 by Joe:

In the 70 percent of Texas public schools where a private curriculum has been installed, students are learning the "fact" that "Allah is the Almighty God," charge critics of a new online curriculum that already is facing condemnation for its secrecy and restrictions on oversight.

The program, called CSCOPE, is a private venture operating under the umbrella of the Texas Education Service Center Curriculum Collaborative, whose incorporation documents state its independence from the State Board of Education of the Texas Education Agency.

In one scenario, students are asked to study the tenets of Islam, and critics say the materials provided exceed impartial review of another faith, extending into requirements of conversion and moral imperatives.

A computer presentation utilized as part of a study of Islam includes information on how to convert, as well as verses denigrating other faiths.

Title: ACT for America Education releases report on Islam in the classroom. Posted on April 4, 2012 by careylj:

The line between "education" and "indoctrination" is, at times, a fine one, and often not a clear one. However, common sense dictates that greater care should be taken to avoid what appears to be indoctrination when the objects of the information are children and youth. Experience demonstrates that children are more malleable than adults. Adults can be reasonably expected to be more able than children to distinguish between objective education and indoctrination.

Therefore, what is taught to children in our public schools should be subjected to a higher standard of scrutiny in order to ensure that what is taking place in the classroom is "education" rather than "indoctrination." This is especially the case when the subject matter is world religions.

This Report does not argue that Islam should not be taught in our public schools. The major religions of the world are one part of our human history, and to exclude teaching about them impedes our understanding of who we are and why the world is at it is.

But when it comes to the teaching of any religion, Islam included, extra care should be exercised by textbook writers and teachers to ensure that what is being taught to their diverse student population is in fact "education" and not "indoctrination." In public schools Muslim parents would no more want their children indoctrinated in Christianity,Judaism or Hinduism than Christian, Jewish or Hindu parents would want their children indoctrinated in Islam –

regardless of whether what amounted to indoctrination was the result of honest mistakes, inattention to detail, ignorance of the subject matter, or bias.

Thus the question posed by this Report. Does the manner in which Islam is generally presented in 6th through 12th grade public school textbooks constitute proper and appropriate education – or does it amount to indoctrination? End of islaminourschools.com articles.

Encroachment by Islamization

According to billionbibles.org Sharia law in the United States of America ("America") has reached Spread of Islam Phase 3. The article explains further:

As the number of court cases that involve conflicts between civil law and Sharia law rise in America, majority of American states have introduced bills banning courts from accommodating Sharia law.

But those bills have been stalled by well-financed challenges in court by Muslim groups that also campaign against politicians who sponsor and/or support such bills. Oklahoma's law banning Sharia law from courts has been struck down, and only seven other conservative states (Louisiana, Arizona, North Carolina, South Dakota, Tennessee, Kansas and Alabama) have been able to pass Sharia law-limiting legislation, and only after watering them to not even mention the word, "Sharia."

While defending the status quo in legislatures, Sharia law has been advancing in other American institutions, including the following:

• An increasing number of public American schools with Muslim students are holding Islamic prayers towards Mecca while public American universities continue to build Muslim-only washing facilities. In 2013, Skokie School District 68 in Illinois became the first US school district to celebrate Eid al-Adha, a Muslim high day, as a school holiday, in lieu of Veterans Day. In 2014, Rocky Mountain High School in Fort Collins, Colorado became the first high school to recite the Pledge of Allegiance in Arabic, replacing "One nation under God," with "One nation under Allah."

• In 1996, Bill Clinton became the first US president to hold an Eid al-Fitr dinner at the White House to celebrate the end of Ramadan, the Muslim month-long dawn-to-dusk fast. Eid al-Fitr includes six "Takbirs," the raising of hands and shouting, "Allahu Akbar!" to declare that Allah, the moon god, is the "Greatest."

• In 2000, the Republican National Convention became the first US presidential convention to open with a Muslim prayer to Allah, the moon god.

• In 2007, Quran for the first time was used to swear into office a new US Congressman, Keith Ellison.

• In 2009, Hudson County Superior Court Judge Joseph Charles Jr. ruled in S.D. v. M.J.R. that the Muslim ex-husband repeatedly had sexually assaulted his Muslim ex-wife, both before and after their divorce. Following testimony from the Muslim man's imam, however, the judge denied the ex-wife's request for a permanent restraining order against her ex-husband, citing the Muslim man's "belief" and "practices": "The court believes that [defendant] was operating under his belief that it is, as the husband, his desire to have sex when and whether he wanted to, was something that was consistent with his practices."

• In 2009, a Christian US soldier at Baghram Air Force Base in Afghanistan received Bibles in two local languages sent by his American church as planned. The US military confiscated those Bibles and instead of at least returning them to the church, burned them. By contrast, when Terry Jones, a pastor in Florida, announced his plan to burn a copy of the Quran in 2010, General David Petraeus, the commander of the US military in Afghanistan, publicly objected to his plan, while US Secretary of State Hillary Clinton denounced his plan as "disgraceful."

• To attract and manage (Middle Eastern) Muslim wealth, an increasing number of American financial institutions are becoming Sharia-compliant. This requires donating a percentage of their annual profits to Islamic organizations designated by their Sharia-compliance advisors, many of whom are members of the Muslim Brotherhood and funnel money to even terrorist groups (donations must go to one or more of eight recipient categories, one of which is Jihad).

• Muslim taxi drivers are challenging local authorities for the right to refuse to pick up blind passengers with seeing-eye dogs, while Muslim supermarket cashiers are challenging their employers for the right to refuse to sell products from pigs. Both are considered unclean in Islam.

Here are the current examples of the continuing Islamization of USA:

Islamization of America

Islamization of America. The Islamization of America is accelerating. In tandem with the spread of Sharia law in America's courts, Islamization of the American media, political and education systems in particular is gaining momentum and confidence, and there is near unanimity that it will continue. The drivers of the accelerating Islamization of America include the following.

Estimated to be five million, the Muslim population in USA today is about the size of the Hispanic population 27 years ago, but it is growing six times faster than the national rate, thanks to high rates of birth, immigration and conversions.

Islam's growth in American prisons is particularly troubling. About 80% of Americans who convert to a religion while in prison become Muslims, who now comprise about 20% of American prison population. The conversion rate is especially high among African-American inmates.

Even more troubling, Islamic groups, including Muslim Brotherhoods' Council on American Islamic Relations (CAIR), have penetrated the highest levels of the US government. The White House now has a White House Muslim Advisor, who has counterpart Muslim advisors at the U.S. Department of Justice, the FBI, and the U.S. Department of Homeland Security, whose Senior Fellow, Mohamed Elibiary recently declared that USA is an "Islamic country".

Members of the Muslim Brotherhood who have penetrated the US government have security clearances and are advising not only on "outreach" programs to the Muslims in the United States but also classified counter-terrorism programs that are supposed to protect Americans from Islamic terrorism. Their recent 'achievements' include:

• Deleting Islam's violent nature and past from FBI counter-terrorism training manuals.

• Blocking the planned indictments of CAIR and other American Muslim Brotherhood organizations listed as unindicted co-conspirators of Holy Land Foundation (HLF), the Muslim Brotherhood "charity" convicted in 2008 of financing Hamas.

• Requiring written communication from and between government agencies to be more "Islam-friendly."

• Pushing for the prosecution of criticizing Islam as hate crimes.

Spread of Islam

The spread of Islam is not a new phenomenon. Ever since Muhammad's troops spread out from Mecca in the 7th century, Islam has been expanding globally. But the spread of Islam in Western democracies is a new trend and one that is gaining momentum.

This spread of Islam in Western nations is led by the Muslim Brotherhood and other international Islamic groups that endeavor to maximize the spread of Sharia law and Islam in the targeted nations while minimizing detection and push-back. This is achieved in five phases:

Spread of Islam Phase 1: Arrival

When the first Muslims arrive in a Western democracy, they keep a low profile and make few if any demands on the host nation. Many quietly work as students, business owners, professors, doctors and other professionals, making good first impressions and gaining vocational respect.

Phase 2: Recognition

When a sufficient number of Muslims gather, they request recognition of the Sharia law being applied within their own community. To preempt resistance and suspicions, they publicly condemn "radical" Islam and even seek well-publicized inter-faith dialogue and gatherings.

They position Islam as a religion of peace whose Sharia law is not a threat to the host nation, especially since it would never be applied outside the Muslim community. Often, they are supported by the host nation's un-informed leaders who are eager to be seen as "progressive".

Phase 3: Penetration

When Muslims gain critical mass in a few cities, they begin to penetrate the host society. They create an alphabet soup of front and umbrella organizations that inflate their reach and unity, and use them to lobby the government, support (pro-)Muslim political candidates, conduct public relations campaigns and file lawsuits against alleged islamophobia, pressure public schools with Muslim students to hold prayers towards Mecca, endow Islamic studies departments at universities, place imams as 'chaplains' in armed forces and prison units.

Sharia The Only Solution Phase 4: Confrontation

When Muslims become a significant minority in the host country, they demand incorporating into its legal system elements of the Sharia law. Often, this demand is made while "rogue" elements from the Muslim community threaten or engage in violence (e.g., Europe and UK).

Phase 5: Imposition

When the Muslim population becomes the majority and/or Islam gains control of a nation (e.g., Taliban in Afghanistan), Sharia law is imposed on the host society, which is then locked down against non-Islamic influences, including Christianity. The ideal Islamic state is Saudi Arabia, where Sharia law is the only law of the land and enforced without mercy. End of article.

Conclusion

D oes Obama not understand that the ultimate tenant of Islam, radical and non-radical, is to make every person 'remaining' on earth a Muslim? Or does he understand it and is part of that process?

Why does he not focus more on American progress, America's future, and the feeling of self worth for every American? Instead, he promises his 'useful innocents' a fair share of America's bounty and blessings, inferring they are unworthy of earning it for themselves. He offers them false hopes of a free ride instead of an opportunity to buy the car for themselves with their own sweat and effort.

Barack Obama is recklessly leading our nation down a dangerous path. He must maintain his large entourage of useful idiots and useful innocents to get to that destination totally foreign to the path set for America by those who designed and planned our magnificent destiny. Hopefully, our wonderful system will work to thwart his goal. That was the purpose for our wonderful Constitution. Will it work?

God bless America.

About the Author

Will Clark's author experiences began by writing inspection and evaluation reports in the U.S. Air Force. He is a retired Air Force officer and a Vietnam veteran, serving in Saigon from 1966 to 1967. His other overseas assignments include Misawa, Japan and Ankara, Turkey.

In 1995, he authored a book, *How to Learn*, as a county-wide study skills project to encourage students to improve their grades in DeSoto County, Mississippi. Education supporters printed and distributed four thousand copies. He also wrote a weekly education column for a local newspaper, *The Desoto County Tribune,* the following school year.

His next published book was *School Bells and Broken Tales*, a parody of nursery rhyme characters, also a motivation and education book for children. His other books include *Shades of Retribution*, a historical novel, and *Simply Success*, a motivation guide for students and employees.

His action novels include a trilogy based on Atlantis and crystals. The first book is titled: *The Atlantis Crystal.* The second book is titled: *She Waits In Atlantis.* The third is: *Return to Atlantis.* This trilogy is based on his travels while assigned to Turkey, site of the ancient city of Troy.

His previous political action novel, *666: Mark of the Beast*, is a sequel to *America 20XX: The New World Order.*

Clark and his wife, Marie, live in Diamondhead, Mississippi, where they play golf with many friends.

Things We Must Never Forget
Until We Know All the Answers

Benghazi

Why were four Americans killed?
Where was Hillary Clinton while it was happening?
Where was Barack Obama while it was happening?
Why did they lie and blame the event on a video?
Why were rescuers on 'stand by' told to 'stand down?'

Fast and Furious

Who authorized the operation?
Why did the operation continue after weapons were lost?
Why did the procedure have no procedure?
Why weren't tracking devices used?

The IRS Scandal

What was the highest level involved?
Who initiated it?
Why hasn't anyone been fired or reprimanded?
What dangers could be unleashed by this organization?

Greatest Quotes
of
Our Time

Michelle Obama
February 18, 2008
"For the first time in my adult life I am proud of my country."
(Age 44)

Barack Obama
March 9, 2008
"We are no longer a Christian nation - at least not just."

September 25, 2012
Remarks to the UN General Assembly
"The future must not belong to those who slander Islam."

Nancy Pelosi
March 9, 2010
"We have to pass the bill so that you can find out what is in it."

Hillary Clinton
January 23, 2013
"What difference, at this point, does it make?"

December 3, 2014
"...showing respect even for one's enemies, trying to understand
and insofar as psychologically possible, empathize with their
perspective and point of view."

Other Books by the Author

Novels:
Shades of Retribution
The Atlantis Crystal
She Waits in Atlantis
Return to Atlantis
America 20XX: The New World Order
666: Mark of the Beast
Death Drones: 2025

Children's Books:
Forest Trails and Fairy Tales
Wishing Wells and Broken Tales
Student Study Skills
American Heroes: Students Who Learn

Non-Fiction:
Simply Success
The Education Jungle
How to Learn
The Day America Died
Obama's Ring: The Seat of Satan
Managing Without Conflict
The Peer Pressure Monster
The War on Christians
Who is the Antichrist
The Seven Spirits
Obama, Hillary, Saul Alinsky and their Useful Idiots